D1557784

TOUCHING THE DISTANCE

NATIVE AMERICAN RIDDLE-POEMS

Brian Swann

ILLUSTRATED BY Maria Rendon

Browndeer Press
Harcourt Brace & Company
San Diego   New York   London

Requests for permission to make copies of any part of the work should be mailed to:
Permissions Department, Harcourt Brace & Company, 6277 Sea Harbor Drive,
Orlando, Florida 32887-6777.

Browndeer Press is a registered trademark of Harcourt Brace & Company.

Library of Congress Cataloging-in-Publication Data
Swann, Brian. Touching the distance: Native American riddle-poems/Brian Swann;
illustrated by Maria Rendon.
p.   cm.
Summary: A collection of brief poems, most only a single line, adapted from the riddles
of various Native American tribes. The illustrations reveal the answers to the riddles.
ISBN 0-15-200804-7
1. Indian riddles—Juvenile poetry.   2. Children's poetry, American.
[1. American poetry.   2. Indian riddles.   3. Riddles.] I. Rendon, Maria, ill.   II. Title.
PS3569.W256T68   1998
811'.54—DC21   96-39354

First edition
A B C D E F

Printed in Singapore

The illustrations in this book are mixed-media constructions.
The display type was set in Bernhard Gothic Medium.
The text type was set in Bernhard Gothic Book.
Transparencies by Artworks, Pasadena, California
Color separations by United Graphic Pte Ltd
Printed and bound by Tien Wah Press, Singapore
This book was printed on totally chlorine-free Nymolla Matte Art paper.
Production supervision by Stanley Redfern
Designed by Judythe Sieck

To Roberta, with love
—B. S.

To Dwight and Papá
—M. R.

A blue calabash

sprinkled

with

toasted

kernels

of

corn

All night   he dances

in a white robe

to all kinds of tunes.

We enter the water
singing,
and we leave the water
singing.

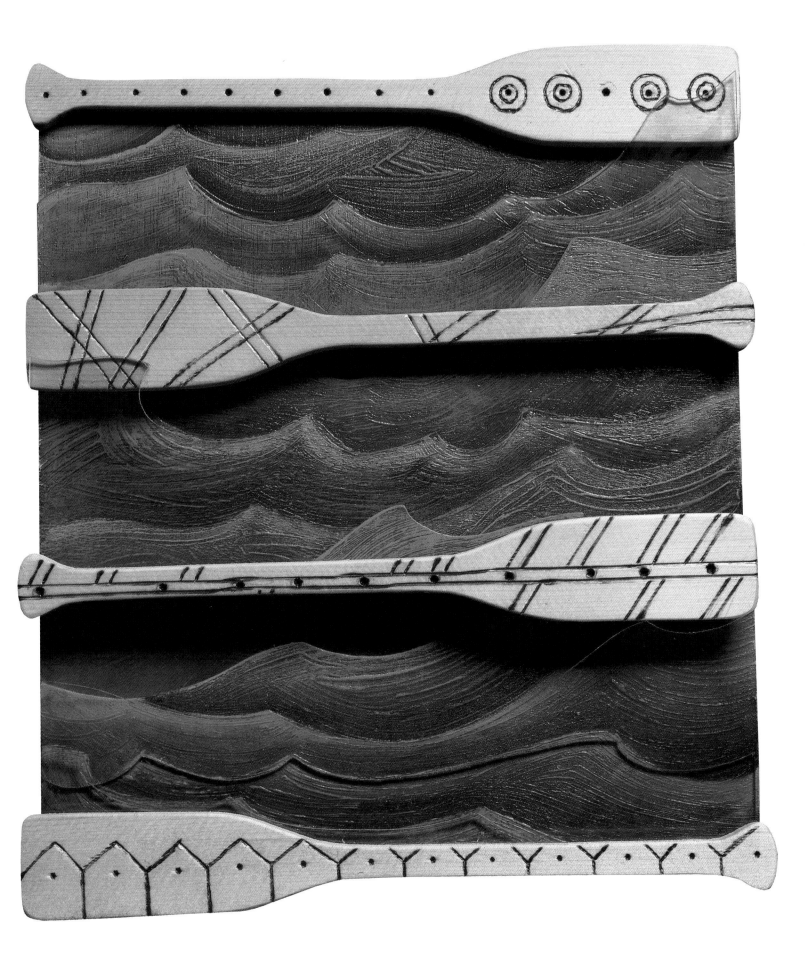

It looks like

a star in the water.

There is a place where a stone sits

in the middle of the water.

I
up ring
fly my
I small
fly up bell
up
I fly
I

My skin is silver,
my heart all gold.

There is that person
whose child will
come out of
her head.

There is
that person
whose child
will come
out of her middle.

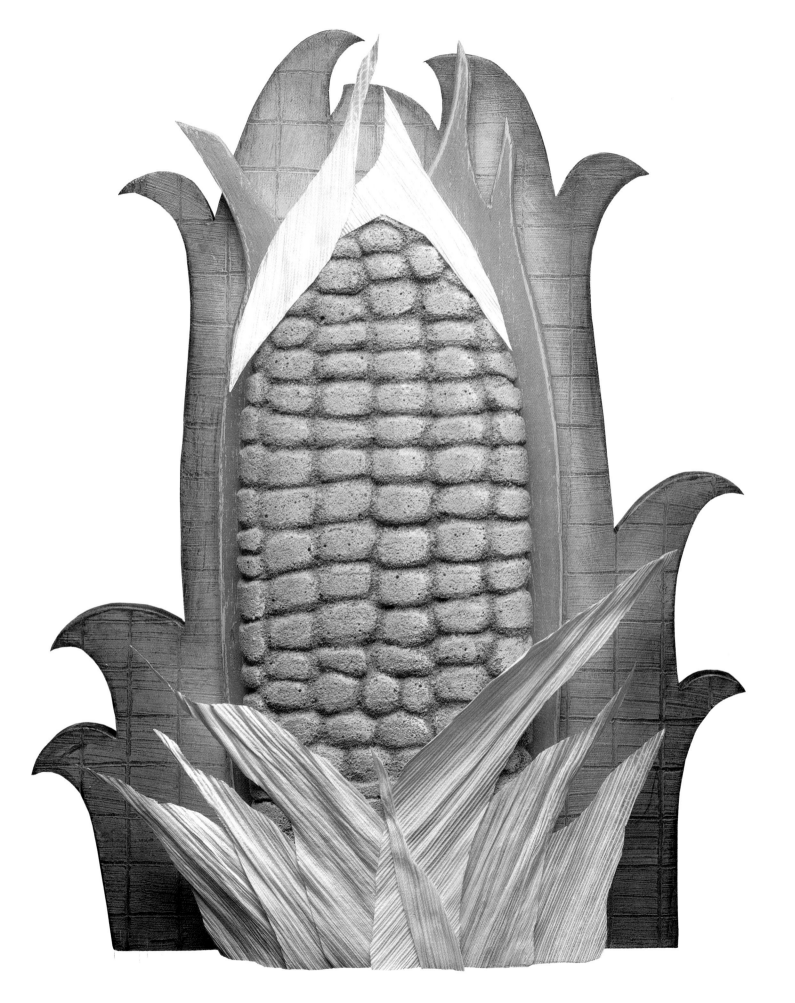

There is that person—if you eat his mouth
he'll eat yours.

I can touch something

far off

in the distance.

There is a place
I know and love well.
It is cut into gullies
where much water fell.

Listen:

    Someone is singing

        a lullaby to children

            in the other world.

Over a rock-pool

a white gourd

sits upside down.

ANSWERS (WITH TRIBES)

Sky with stars (Aztec—Mexico)

Moth (Chipaya—Southwest Bolivia)

Paddles (Ten'a—Alaska)

Eye of a fish (Amizgo—Mexico)

Turtle (Amizgo—Mexico)

Mosquito (Ten'a—Alaska)

Egg (Mayan—Mexico)

Banana plant (Amizgo—Mexico)

Corn (Amizgo—Mexico)

Chili pepper (Amizgo—Mexico)

Eyesight (Koyukon—Alaska)

My grandmother's face (Omaha)

Fast-moving current (Koyukon—Alaska)

Moonrise (Mayan—Mexico)

ACKNOWLEDGMENTS

The riddles in this book are new poems drawn from the following sources.

Sky with stars
Bernardo de Sahagún. *Historia general de las cosas de Nueva España.* Sixteenth century. Reprint, Barcelona: Tusquets Editores, 1985.

Moth
Charles T. Scott. "New Evidence of Native American Riddles," *Journal of American Folklore,* 2d ser., 76 (July–September 1963).

Paddles, mosquito
Julius Jette. "Riddles of the Ten'a Indians," *Anthropos* VIII (1913).

Eye of a fish, turtle, banana plant, corn, chili pepper
Charles T. Scott. "A Linguistic Study of Persian and Arabic Riddles: A Language-Centered Approach to Genre Definition." Ph.D. dissertation, University of Texas, 1963.

Egg, moonrise
Margaret Park Redfield. "The Folk Literature of a Yucatecan Town," *Carnegie Institute Contributions to American Archeology* III, nos. 13-19 (1937).

Eyesight, fast-moving current
Eliza Jones, translator and transcriber. *K'ooltsaah Ts'in': Koyukon Riddles Told by Chief Henry.* Fairbanks, Alaska: Alaskan Native Language Center, University of Alaska, 1976.

My grandmother's face
Archer Taylor. "American Indian Riddles," *Journal of American Folklore* 57 (1944).

~~Edgewood~~ Public Montessori LMC
Okemos, MI